MW01147167

STAY RICH
— *with a* —
BALANCED PORTFOLIO

STAY RICH
— *with a* —
BALANCED PORTFOLIO

The Price You Pay for Peace of Mind

J. TED OAKLEY

RIVER GROVE
BOOKS

This publication is designed to provide accurate and authoritative information in regard to the subject matter covered. It is sold with the understanding that the publisher and author are not engaged in rendering legal, accounting, or other professional services. Nothing herein shall create an attorney-client relationship, and nothing herein shall constitute legal advice or a solicitation to offer legal advice. If legal advice or other expert assistance is required, the services of a competent professional should be sought.

The testimonial provided by Dan Kennedy on the back cover was provided by a current client of Oxbow Advisors on July 25, 2023. The client was not compensated, nor are there material conflicts of interest that would affect the given statement. The statement may not be representative of the experience of other current clients and does not provide a guarantee of future performance success or similar services.

Published by River Grove Books
Austin, TX
www.rivergrovebooks.com

Copyright © 2023 Oxbow Advisors

All rights reserved.

Thank you for purchasing an authorized edition of this book and for complying with copyright law. No part of this book may be reproduced, stored in a retrieval system, or transmitted by any means, electronic, mechanical, photocopying, recording, or otherwise, without written permission from the copyright holder.

Distributed by River Grove Books

Design and composition by Greenleaf Book Group and Mimi Bark
Cover design by Greenleaf Book Group and Mimi Bark
Cover image used under license from ©Shutterstock.com/Isa H

Publisher's Cataloging-in-Publication data is available.

Print ISBN: 978-1-63299-767-8

eBook ISBN: 978-1-63299-768-5

First Edition

OXBOW ADVISORS

AT OXBOW ADVISORS, we've spent thirty-five years working with people who have gained significant first-generation wealth and are trying to maximize it across future generations.

Many of these individuals have experienced liquidity events, and they depend on our extensive knowledge to help them navigate their way to long-term security and an enduring financial legacy.

What we do is simple but hard to find in today's investment world: we protect the wealth you worked hard to create.

If you would like more information, call 512-386-1088 or visit www.OxbowAdvisors.com.

CONTENTS

THE CASE
FOR BALANCE

Over more than thirty-five years of working with investors, I've come to recognize—and anticipate—the patterns that cause their worst anxieties and fears.

The one factor that weighs most on investor peace of mind is *balance*. It seems like such a simple premise—just a comfortable, equitable relationship between elements. We seek it in every area of our lives—between work and rest, between health and indulgence, between being aggressive and being passive. But balance isn't always easy to find or choose—especially when it comes to money. Somehow a lot of people have a much harder time saying no to risky investments than they do to an extra slice of cake or one too many cocktails—even though the fallout of one terrible investment mistake can last a lifetime.

I suspect the reason so many investors struggle with finding balance has to do with common misconceptions that find their way to them every day. You get an earful when someone you know makes a killing in the market, for example. But most of your friends and colleagues don't mention when they take a dramatic loss. You hear about big financial moves and get stock tips—right alongside millions of other listeners and viewers tuned in to the 24-hour news cycle. If you have substantial wealth, chances are you also have people lined up at the fringes of your life offering "rare," "privileged," and "once-in-a-lifetime" opportunities to make far more money. And let's not forget the oversimplified understanding that the stock market inevitably goes up. That may be true, but it doesn't go up in a straight line, and what if you happen to invest during a one-, five-, or ten-year dry spell? Or just in a collection of stocks that dwindle to nothing? Well, the fact that one day the market will go up again won't be much consolation.

Here's the bare-bones truth: If you are an investor, somewhere along the line you need to get settled with the way you manage your assets, finding the balance that allows you to both achieve gains *and* be at ease with your strategy. If you don't, you'll end up an emotional mess—always looking back, wondering *what if*, bogged down with regret. You could spend years chasing and losing. That's not just a worst-case scenario—it's a reality I see investors living every day.

At Oxbow Advisors, the firm I founded to create a grounded, expert alternative to Wall Street's smoke-and-mirrors investment mentality, we've spent decades studying the foundations of financial peace of mind. We've focused on coming up with logical, measured approaches that put those fears to bed. The key to finding both peace and prosperity in investing comes down to choosing a balanced approach. That means sometimes you won't make the most dramatic gains—but neither will you get financially bludgeoned when the market takes a dive. Being balanced will help you sleep at night. It'll help you live your life unencumbered by anxiety over money. And it'll allow you to demonstrate what being comfortable with investment strategy looks like to your children and grandchildren (and believe me, they are watching and picking up your habits).

The majority of investors are a little (or a lot) out of balance—either because they're operating from emotion, using a failing strategy, or choosing to only know what their investment advisors tell them. In the chapters that follow, I hope you can gain enough knowledge to feel more in charge of your strategy and more balanced in it.

The truth is, Wall Street is in the business of giving you good news, of keeping you hopeful. That's how it makes money. A truly responsible financial advisor, however, is in the business of ensuring you *keep* your wealth. At Oxbow, we specialize in providing this service for investors who have significant assets. Since the start of the company, we've had a special affinity for business owners who've sold their companies and are transitioning between two sets of priorities: from building and growing the business and its profits to safeguarding and cultivating that wealth so it can serve their families indefinitely. Over our long experience, we've developed a deep understanding of investment principles, of common misconceptions, and of a uniquely balanced approach.

In the chapters that follow, we'll take a look at the concepts and strategies every investor should consider in the continuous quest for financial balance and the confidence that comes with it.

Part 1

A DOSE OF COMMON SENSE

CHAPTER 1

THERE IS NO HOLY GRAIL

I f there's one lesson a long career in finance teaches, it's to never get complacent. Just when investors start to forget every bull ultimately meets a bear, or that inflation can upend the best-laid plans, or that interest rates go up as well as down—reality comes calling. The truth is, there's no single investment class that wins all the time—no financial Holy Grail. You can search high and low. A lot of people do, but it doesn't exist.

Most investors get into trouble after doing well in something and deciding they've found an unbeatable investment. For most people from 2010–2021, that something was stocks that climbed as if they'd never find a ceiling. Or maybe you've prospered in bonds. Or real estate. Or new business start-ups. During some stretches of time, they're all winning hands.

But whatever your favorite investment, whatever one has served you well, the day comes when it slows, or even crashes. This is why seasoned wealth advisors preach diversification. Unfortunately, just like anybody who takes to the pulpit, they're often speaking to audiences daydreaming about more exciting things—like dollar signs. The problem with those big dreams is that they neglect the single biggest tenet of investment: *don't lose money*.

At Oxbow, we often welcome new investors through our doors after they've gone through a liquidity event—the sale of a business, the signing of a significant contract, the receipt of a big inheritance, or even winning the lottery. These individuals with newly liquid wealth seek guidance on how to protect and grow their fortunes—a wise way to start out a period of new wealth. But there's another contingent of new clients who decide to seek investment counsel—the ones who show up *after* suffering spectacular losses. For many, those losses can be directly attributed to "chasing" strategies—chasing headlines, chasing other people's successes, chasing more and faster returns—all with disastrous results.

Consider an example: some years ago, I worked with a gentleman tasked with overseeing significant investments for an elderly family member. For nearly two decades this man was tied to directives from that elder for conservative, protective investments—a choice we at Oxbow followed and used to ensure not just the safekeeping of her wealth but also a steady income that covered her living expenses. When this woman passed away and her steward gained a free hand with those investments, he came to us at the top of the market and insisted the family money be invested more aggressively. We advised against it; he pressed on. In a stretch of just a few months, he lost a crushing 35 percent of the family's wealth. A year later, with the market down and bargains finally available, he was scared to death because of how much he'd already lost. So he once again pushed the wrong way, this time insisting on extremely conservative moves.

Like countless investors before him, a lack of balance put this man's portfolio behind the eight ball, not just some of the time, but all of the time. No amount of logic could convince him that by the time he saw any investment tip on the news or in some financial blog, the action point had already passed.

WHAT BALANCE LOOKS LIKE

Faced with the impossibility of a sure-thing investment, how does a balanced portfolio protect you, and what does it look like? Let's talk protection first. Unless you are willing to accept great risk, you need balance to ensure you can't get slowly drained or quickly wiped out by any single investment failing. To illustrate just how much of a role fate plays, I often share a hypothetical with investors in which an individual begins with $5 million and withdraws

4 percent of that fund each year. Based on historic market performance, if that investment was made in 2000, by 2021 the investor would have a remaining principal balance of just over $2 million.

If you simply reverse the order of returns—using historic market performance in the opposite order (2021–2000), the same $5 million investor winds up with a principal balance of almost $16 million after twenty-one years.

In each case, the investor was at the mercy of a single investment vehicle (in this case, stocks) and critically impacted by starting point. Investor A stayed afloat but faced diminished withdrawals. Investor B won big and was set for decades to come.

And there's your trouble: the fate of those fortunes was largely left to luck. Those two outcomes were almost entirely predicated on factors that were out of the investors' control.

So how do you take control? In Part 2, I'll delve into specific strategies, but the big picture here is that a truly balanced portfolio is multifaceted, including the obvious components of stocks and bonds but also less-discussed assets in the form of income-producing investments and cash on hand. That combination would have meant a higher return and a larger ending balance for Investor A in that twenty-one-year investment scenario, and it would have meant a lower return and remaining balance for Investor B. Of course, we'd all like to be Investor B, getting in at the right time to maximize returns, but the cost of financial and emotional calm is mitigating your exposure to risk—choosing balance. Doing so makes you a different kind of investor entirely—one whose fortunes don't rise or fall at the whim of the market alone.

Nobody likes to leave money on the table, and nobody likes to lose their shirt. At Oxbow, we've long built our business on guiding investors to protect the wealth they have and use it to support their lifestyles. Every day we meet new investors who come to us—many of them after taking a financial beating—looking for something that's become a rare commodity in the investment world: *common sense*.

CHAPTER 2

WHY YOUR
HISTORY MATTERS

Some of the biggest predictors of investor behavior come down to when the individual was born, their formative experiences with finance, the extent to which they can manage emotional reactions, their investing track record, and how much they have to lose. If you're working on becoming a steadier, more balanced investor, the first thing you need to do is take a hard look at your own history as it pertains to these elements and make peace with it.

Let's take a look at each factor.

AGE

Perhaps the single biggest factor in how an investor views stocks is the era in which they grew up and first became aware of finances. For example, in the past I've worked with investors who lived through the Great Depression. Most of them never owned stock again—they were disgusted at the very idea of it.

By the 1950s, stocks were trusted investment vehicles again, and people who came to investing during that decade tend to view them with rose-colored glasses.

My own experience of this goes all the way back to 1974, when I got out of college. If you were there with me or came into investing anytime during the decade that came after, chances are you're extremely guarded about risk. During that stretch, an inflation rate that varied between 5 percent and nearly 15 percent strained both consumers and investors, and it made a lasting impression.

And, of course, if you got your first taste of stock investment anytime between 2010 and 2021, there's a good chance you came into 2022 thinking you and your investments were infallible. Stocks were an old friend who'd never let you down.

The point is, every investor should be aware that their age and their generation's experience with stocks, bonds, real estate, interest rates, and inflation are all filters through which you view options and make choices.

LIFE EXPERIENCE

Your overall life experience constantly influences your investment views, but nothing carries quite as much weight for most people as the relationship they built with money when they were growing up.

As someone who grew up in deep poverty, and also as someone who's worked with young people who've never known a minute's want (or work) in their lives, I've seen this play out on every possible level. Where you were and what you saw, what you learned about money as a child, as a teen, as a young adult—those things shaped your investment mentality.

For someone like me who grew up lacking even the most basic necessities, money became synonymous with security. Because I had to work relentlessly to achieve that security, I've never taken the freedom that comes with wealth for granted, not even for a minute.

Many of Oxbow's investors who come to investing after selling companies they built from scratch share this experience and a similar perspective on wealth. They know how hard a person might have to work to earn a dollar or a million dollars, and they are mindful of seeing others who have not been successful or who've lost everything.

At the other end of the spectrum are people for whom money is just an old, reliable pal. Sometimes they're simply from wealthy backgrounds or too young to have experienced any kind of loss. Sometimes they've gone through life thus far with fortune smiling on them (often combined with their hard work and smart choices). This group is often the hardest hit when they take on too much risk and an investment fails. They can't believe it could happen to them. Shockingly, some of them are so convinced of this that they will double down and lose again.

One of my other books, *$20 Million and Broke*, looks at some of the myriad ways the individuals in this group—many of them extremely accomplished entrepreneurs—manage to wipe out their wealth with this mentality.

The key here is recognizing that your lifetime experience with money—especially in your youth—is a lens that influences your choices. If you're not cognizant of that fact, your past experiences may loom over every investment decision you make. They may drive you to be overly aggressive or overly conservative. They may compel you to complicate things that should be simple. They may cause you to worry day and night about the state of your investments. None of those things will help your strategy or help you achieve balance. All of them have the potential to do you harm.

EMOTIONAL TIES TO MONEY

This topic cuts across both broad investment mentality and deeply personal feelings about wealth. For starters, one factor that weighs on just about everyone's relationship with money is whether they accept the fact that *investment*—keeping and holding the assets you have—is a fundamentally different undertaking from building a business. Business owners are on *offense*—building, expanding, and creating wealth through innovation, maneuvering, and plain old hard work. Investors are on *defense*—their primary occupation should always be protecting their wealth and ensuring it will generate enough income to cover their cost of living.

Business owners who can't take a step back from the grow-or-die approaches that fueled their entrepreneurial efforts are far less likely to seek and maintain investment balance than their peers who recognize that wealth preservation requires a level, measured approach.

For many, this macro-level of emotional connection is just the beginning. Over the years, I've met an awful lot of people who have extremely unhealthy relationships with wealth—both those who can't be secure at any number and those who simply go by faith that money will appear when they need it. There are those who let ego drive their every investment decision and those who let fear push them to stay out of balance—investing too little or too much in the market or holding it in cash or stocks that are stuck in the mud. And then there are those who take a single loss and then spend the rest of their investment lives worrying about the next.

Other problematic emotional profiles include people with "investor dementia" (individuals who are quick to forget past losses) and those who become consumed with regrets. If you get into trouble, what you need is a reset and a reliable advisor. What you don't need is to pine over what's gone. You can't put it back, and you can't undo the past. The only viable next step is choosing to focus on the future.

At Oxbow, we do extensive work with investors to nail down their risk proclivity before guiding major investment decisions. Time and again, we see the problem of overreaction in play. Unfortunately, a lot of people aren't able to truly answer questions about this until they've been through a loss. Many can go along with their investments thinking one day they might stub their toe taking some small loss, but they don't understand that losses can be sudden and far more severe.

At a minimum, each investor needs to consider how they'd handle a drop of 20–30 percent—not all that uncommon an event in stocks. If you don't believe that can happen—or can't deal with it when it does—you need to be doubly committed to taking a balanced investment approach.

The fact is, the only way to overcome the potentially blinding power of your emotional relationship with wealth is to build a balanced portfolio that shields you from the most volatility while still doing the critical job of keeping you ahead of inflation.

YOUR INVESTING TRACK RECORD

Just as you should consider where you come from when you look at what it'll take for you to achieve balance in investing, also consider what you've done so far. Sometimes your true colors when it comes to these things are most evident in your previous actions. That's why I always ask investors how they handled previous financial crises. For many, the answers reveal panic, remorse, and uncertainty about their choices. Part of that has to do with actual poor choices, and part of it with a fundamental lack of understanding of how investment works and what anyone who's in the market must be prepared to endure.

Have you been jumping around from strategy to strategy, alternately running from your fears and chasing after pots of gold? Or have you been steady? Investors need to be honest with themselves (and with their advisors) when it comes to this, because if the volatility of certain investments is intolerable to you, that needs to be factored into every decision regarding your portfolio. Every time the stock market takes a dive, I know some frazzled investor will call and tell us to sell everything they've got—at the bottom. When things start to look up again, these are inevitably the same people who want to hop on the roller coaster when it's already halfway—or more—up its climb. That investor would have been better off staying out of stocks entirely than continuing in a cycle of fear, panic, greed, and loss.

Fortunes are protected and grown by those who stay long enough to see their choices through. Those who chase and jump around, pulled by their emotions rather than their intellect, are doomed to struggle.

Not sure where you stand? Consider these questions:

- Have you experienced a market downturn? Did it impact your daily life or your sleep?

- How have you reacted in prior bear markets? Did you panic and liquidate? Did you then agonize over when and how to get back in?

- Do you have the ability to buy more when investments are down?

One more key factor about your investment history is that if you're young, you have a lot more latitude when it comes to being out of balance and heavily in the market. If you've got twenty to forty years ahead before you plan to draw on your investment wealth, you can weather a lot of storms along the way. But if you're fifty-five or sixty, looking at retiring and living off investments alone in a few years, then being out of balance in a downturn can potentially devastate your plans. The older you are, the more balance matters—and the more you should be sitting back on slow, steady growth rather than chasing exponential but risky returns.

If any of this is alarming to you, or if you've been through a significant loss, consider seeking professional help to do a reset and calibrate your investments. Do not trust your assets to anyone offering you a get-rich-quick scheme (and there are a lot of these). Any investment advisor worth your time should start out by telling you how they will *preserve* your wealth and then move on to sharing how they can build it and ensure it generates income for the long term.

PORTFOLIO SIZE

Portfolio size is an investment factor we don't talk about enough. The fact is, the bigger the portfolio, the more an investor is able to weather short-term losses (and longer-term ones as well). If you have $20 million, $100 million, or more, in most cases you have a fairly substantial cash level (or at least you should). That makes it easier to stay calm and wait out market extremes. Among investors with $2 million or less, however, most are quick to get nervous at any loss. They have good reason if they haven't got a cushion to protect them from a drop. For these investors it is doubly important to find the right investment balance. Many come to investing determined to see great growth—to stay all in, all the time—and also to assume no risk. Unfortunately, that combination doesn't happen here on earth.

OXBOW NOTE

In my book *$20 Million and Broke*, I outline the reasons wealth loss is so common using real-life examples. If you'd like a complimentary copy of this book or any of my other titles, contact us at www.OxbowAdvisors.com.

CHAPTER 3

HOW BIAS
IMPACTS BALANCE

M any investors are not balanced due to their biases. It's unfortunate because those biases hinder what could be an overall healthy approach to investing. Where does that bias come from? In most cases it goes back to those experiences we talked about in chapter 2—how you grew up and early situations that might not have been the norm. One of the most important lessons we teach to our young portfolio managers at Oxbow is to recognize and strive to overcome their own biases. Why is that important? Because no one approach can consistently be correct. The investment world isn't static, and as it constantly changes, sometimes you need to be more aggressive and at other times more conservative. If you're tied to a psychological bias about either approach, you won't be able to shift when you need to and trust the outcome.

Over the years, there are a few biased attitudes I've encountered time and again. Investors should consider whether they see themselves in these profiles and if maybe they have biases of their own to overcome.

BIAS #1: FEAR

The group with this bias is constantly protecting, protecting, protecting—always afraid to take risks because at times the prices may go against them. These people are so guarded that they miss out on some of the best investment opportunities. They believe their money will run out—no matter how much they start with or how well they manage it.

Deep down, this group believes everything is eventually going to go badly. They maintain overly defensive positions in order to have a sense of control, but the truth is, none of us has that kind of control—not over anything. You can eat healthy, but you might still get sick. You can drive safely, but you could still get in an accident. Of course, you can (and should) take measures to be responsible and cautious, but you can't account for every single risk. Obsessing about being safe just isn't the same thing as actually being safe.

Most people with this fear of running out of money have carried it with them all their lives. It was shaped by early experiences when they went without. As someone who grew up in extreme poverty, I know what it's like to carry this conservative bias. It took me twenty years in the business world to learn to move past it. Once I did, though, I felt the relief of being free from worry. It wasn't that I didn't want to (or choose to) practice good money habits. It was the realization that to get returns, I needed to accept risk. Balanced risk, which we'll get into more in the coming chapters, is the level at which you can learn to feel secure.

BIAS #2: EXCESS

This group of people has little respect for money. They're the careless and the big spenders. They take inordinate risks and never think about consequences. The possibility of running down their capital never crosses their minds—at least not until the damage is done.

Many times, I've seen a business owner sell a company and go on a spending spree with absolutely no regard for future cash flows. What happens is this: they make too many illiquid and even frivolous investments, and they keep doing it until they don't have enough cash-producing assets to support their lifestyle. You don't get cash flow from a new jet. You don't get cash flow from a $10 million house in Aspen. Quite the opposite—those investments tie up assets that should be generating cash in perpetuity.

This same group tends to be far too gullible when people come to them with "opportunities" that supposedly have no risk and unlimited upside—even though those opportunities rarely exist. Not surprisingly, many members of this group are obsessed with having all the right things: yachts, planes, vacation homes, accounts in all the right places, seats on all the right boards. They do it for the bragging rights, and they rarely, if ever, find the happiness they're ceaselessly trying to buy.

BIAS #3: SACRIFICE

We have investors from time to time who sacrifice everything for their children—even when no such sacrifice is necessary. This group is fixated on legacy and on the dependence of their dependents. As a result, they are uber-conservative in their investment choices, staying passive in times when aggressive investment could bring them great deals.

The guiding principle for this group is always about making sure the kids are okay—even when those "kids" are decades into adulthood. What these investors fail to realize is that the children *will* be okay, will thrive—but only if they learn to stand on their own feet and become self-sufficient.

Life is meant for living now, not next year or at some future date. Members of this group, who all too often feel they need to martyr themselves for the security of the next generation, would do well to focus a little more on the joys and possibilities of their own lifetimes and a little less on what's going to happen in the far-distant future.

BIAS #4: ABJECT LOYALTY

This is a tricky one. Over the many decades I've helped wealthy investors, there is one group that has a unique loyalty problem. They're a contingent who got rich owning stock in a company they worked for. Often the stock was part of their compensation package, and at some point it became worth much more than they ever thought they'd see. As a result, they end up with a high percentage of their net worth in one security. This can also happen with investors who have family ties to a corporation or who simply become fixated on an individual company.

It's hard for people in this group to part with any of their personal-favorite stock because it has made them a great deal of money. I like a couple of different approaches to dealing with this paralyzing problem. The first is "dollar-cost selling," which is the opposite of dollar-cost averaging when buying stock. In dollar-cost averaging, you buy your stock in increments over a long period of time in order to lessen the impact of market volatility. In dollar-cost selling, you reduce your stock holding in the same way—selling on the way up as the price reaches certain points. The fact is, anyone with more than 50 percent of their liquid net worth in one stock is overweight on it. It's rare to find any valid reason for staying that high.

At Oxbow, we recommend picking a number (for example, 25 percent of liquid net worth) and selling everything above that figure. Then each year, once again sell the amount above your hold number. This simple practice will keep that beloved stock from occupying a dangerously large portion of your portfolio.

The second way to address a portfolio that's overweight with a favorite stock is by selling covered stock options. The way this works is simple and effective—if you own a stock and sell its option at a higher price (for example, a six-month option for a 100-share block to move from $56 per share to $60). In doing so, you gain the option cost as income if the stock doesn't go up. You can continually renew those options to create ongoing revenue. If the stock *does* go up, you retain the right to buy it back and can then sell at the higher price. Either way, this is an investment tool that helps generate some cash flow. It may also make it a little easier to part with shares when you're holding too much of a single security.

It is far too common an occurrence for stocks to go full circle and end up with a deep downside. Anyone with a strong bias for a single security should consider whether they really love it enough to put their financial health at risk by holding on to it. If not, it's time to diversify with one of these methods.

Part 2

ESSENTIAL COMPONENTS OF A BALANCED PORTFOLIO

CHAPTER 4

THE ROLE OF STOCKS

Stocks are the only investment category that can be counted on to hold up against inflation over the long term. That's why most investors need them. After a long stretch of low inflation through 2021, investors (and consumers) got a serious taste of the damage higher rates can do to their buying power in 2022 and beyond. Consider this: if you have a million-dollar portfolio and inflation stays flat at 4 percent, in ten years you'll need $1,480,000 to buy the exact same things you'd purchase today for your million.

Staying out of the market typically means failing to keep up with the cost of living, and investors who refuse to accept any volatility tend to look up after a decade or so and realize they've fallen behind. I've worked with investors who were slow to admit they'd spent too much money while ignoring these facts—ultimately putting them in positions where they had to dip into protected capital, sell houses, or cut their expenditures to continue to live off their wealth.

THE INSECURITY PROBLEM

The catch is this: your ticket to the stock market is volatility. Stocks are the component of a balanced approach that can keep investors up at night. Markets can swing 10, 20, or 30 percent in a matter of a day or a week, and dividends are never going to cover that kind of loss. There is some protection against this in choosing quality stocks that have strong earnings, growth potential, and deep pockets—but there is no way to entirely sidestep market risks.

When new investors sit down with us at Oxbow, we make sure they know that on a number of occasions over the last sixty years, the market has fallen 35–40 percent or more. When you choose how much of your wealth you intend to invest in the market, you have to believe that can happen, and you have to be able to emotionally withstand that reality if it comes to pass. Because if you don't, you'll do something irrational. You'll get depressed. You'll duck out at the bottom. You'll move funds that are supposed to be locked in for years. And any or all of those moves will be to the detriment of your own long-term bottom line.

This is the biggest reason why balance is key. If you are balanced when the bottom falls out of the stock market, with an asset mix of stocks, bonds, cash, and income-producing investments, then you'll be able to get through it, to feel good about your investment decisions, and rest easy. A balanced portfolio won't get wiped out, and it won't take as long to recover from a tough blow to the markets.

THE FUNDAMENTALS

In all the excitement and the detachment of stock trading, investors sometimes lose sight of the fact that as a shareholder, they own a piece of a real company that may do well, may stagnate, or may even fall apart. When you buy a share, you buy equity. That puts you on equal footing with everyone else who owns that security, from the largest shareholder to the owner of just one share. And you are making a leap of faith with your purchase—both on the profitability of the company and the strength of the overall economy. Whether you choose stocks across a broad base of industries and companies or engage a skilled money manager to do so, your investments should reflect this shared ownership. That means choosing companies that actually make something, sell something, or provide a service with inherent value.

At Oxbow, for example, we own excellent companies— companies that prove it out with earnings and revenues. We don't just bet on companies that *might*, *possibly*, *eventually* make money—something far too many fund managers do. That's not sound strategy. We have a holding period of five to fifteen years, and in order to earn their way into our holdings, companies have to be demonstrably stable, strong, and profitable.

This may sound too simple to mention, but I assure you I meet investors every day who've been drawn in by sales pitches or news stories or even well-placed rumors. They've bought into companies that have never actually made any money. Many of those corporations, including a contingent of well-known tech businesses, can dazzle with billion-dollar revenue numbers, but when you look past their complex and skewed calculations, you won't find a hint of commensurate net incomes.

COMMON PITFALLS

The upsides of stock investment are obvious: their average returns beat any of your other investment options. At times, they're the only thing that can keep up with inflation. Used wisely, they can increase wealth year over year—*most* of the time. But there are concerns, and every investor should go into this kind of invest- ment with their eyes wide open. Consider the following potentially troubling (and costly) scenarios:

"Playing" the market

References to playing, gambling, betting, dabbling—they all represent the worst way to go about stock investment. The long-term management of substantial wealth is a highly complex business, not a casino game or a hobby. Despite all the ways people compare them, investing in the stock market has almost nothing in common with betting on a horse, rolling the dice on a craps table, or getting dealt into a high-stakes poker game. Those activities are entertainment—same as going to the movies or attending a ball game. Stock investment is a key component in managing the entirety of your financial future. It requires sound strategy and real expertise. And it typically requires professional advisors who prioritize being good stewards of your money.

At Oxbow, we frequently encounter investors who are handpicking stocks, playing the market like they might play a Monopoly board. That is, in all honesty, the worst way to go about stock investment. If you must own single stocks, spread them over fifteen to twenty companies or more and make sure they are diversified by both industry and company. This is an area where a professional money manager can really help you.

Going all in, all at once

You can do everything right and still lose a fortune in the stock market if you choose to drop everything in it all at once. Starting point matters. It is profoundly important. For every sky-high run the market makes, there's an ugly dip, and you can no sooner pinpoint each of these than you can choose winning lottery numbers. There are too many factors in play.

For example, if you dropped your life's savings into the S&P 500 in March of 2000, it likely took you all the way until April of 2013 to break even. But if you started in 2009 and got out in 2021—well, you were on board for high, after high, after high.

At Oxbow, we never advise any investor to go all in at once. Invest a little at a time, month over month, then year over year. If market conditions start to deteriorate, slow down. This is not a plow-ahead situation—it's a slow, steady process. When you do that, you're working with average levels, and history and market trends will be on your side.

Getting sentimental

A lot of people get caught up in a specific stock with the big idea that they're going to buy low and make a killing. That's a good way to lose a fortune. If you choose three stocks, for example, and invest a third of your portfolio in each—well, then you have to be almost perfect in your choices. If even just one of those stocks tanks, it'll pull down your whole portfolio. A wise market investment is not an individual stock investment—it's an investment in the entire economy.

This is a conversation I often need to have with people who have stock in their own companies. Seems like a great idea in theory—certainly there's no other company you know more about—but in reality, no matter how much you like your company, you can't take the risk of having too much concentration of wealth in any single asset. It's a huge gamble.

A worst-case scenario of this played out here in Texas some time ago, back when Enron was a darling stock in Houston. I knew many individuals who worked for the company and had their 401(k)s invested in company stock. At its peak in the late summer of 2000, Enron shares were trading at just over $90 a share. There were a lot of 401(k) millionaires holding on to that stock. But by the end of 2001, the shares were worthless. Ninety to zero is a long way to fall, but it can absolutely happen. The thousands of investors who were holding disproportionate volumes of their company's stock suffered financial setbacks that would echo through the rest of their lives. Enron is a memorable example, but the fact is, dramatic stock flameouts happen all the time. Most of them just don't receive quite so much public fanfare.

The danger of getting sentimental may be the single most compelling argument against handpicking individual stocks. When you've gone through that process and bought in, it's easy to become emotionally tied to the idea of the company and its possible success, and it may make it difficult to see it strictly as an investment. Individual stocks = emotional ties.

Holding on too long or not long enough

If you bought Merck stock in 1994, it was trading around $12 per share. By the first quarter of 2000, it had climbed to over $82 per share—demonstrating great growth for its stockholders. Knowing that, can you guess how the stock of this viable company with a recognizable name was priced in March of 2022?

It was at $82 per share. Despite some moderate ups and downs along the way, the share price had taken *twenty-two years* to return to its 2000 level.

I've known many investors who've held the stock (and plenty of others with similar performance records) decade, after decade, after decade. Why? Because of that first big $70 run. In many investors' minds, a stock that's made them money is *always* a winner. Perhaps they were receiving a small dividend, but they could have generated that extremely low-level return in a stable investment, like a treasury bond. Stocks that don't climb over decades don't serve the purpose of stock investment—because they don't beat inflation.

The key here is that even though you've probably heard all your life that the best investor buys stocks and simply *holds* them, there is far more to smart investment than putting stocks on the shelf and leaving them to grow. Many stocks don't grow, or they grow and then shrink, or they die altogether.

By the way, some investors know this and *still* hang on to their underperforming shares to avoid taxes on long-ago gains. This is nonsensical logic. You want to be invested in stocks that are getting you a return. If getting there means paying taxes, so be it—it means you made money. That beats sitting on stagnant securities every time.

Part of finding the right balance in your stock portfolio and in your overall investment strategy is regular assessment and reallocation. Are your stocks performing? Are they paying dividends? Is the overall calculation a loss? Don't just sit on something indefinitely because once upon a time it made you some money.

STOCKS IN BALANCE

Wondering how much is too much? The question every investor must consider comes down to just how deep they want to be in stocks. What's the right amount to let you benefit from the market's upside without taking on an intolerable or inadvisable amount of risk? Consider these factors:

1. *Age*: In general, the older you are, the less you need to (or should) keep in stocks. If you're over seventy and you have enough funds to support your lifestyle with some inflation for the next twenty years, then there's no reason for you to put your principal at risk. Conversely, if you're thirty and you've got multiple streams of income, then you can afford to be more aggressive in stocks and trust that in the extreme long term the market will bear out.

There's an old but relevant adage for stock investment that suggests the percentage of your assets in stocks should be equal to 100 minus your age. The biggest issue with this guidance is that it first started being used in the 1950s, and since then life expectancies have steadily gone up by more than ten years. To account for this significant difference, 110 minus your age may be a more useful general parameter. But know it's just a guideline. There will never be a simple plug-and-play formula that factors in all the nuances of your financial situation and your psychological tolerance for risk. For that you'll need to work with seasoned advisors who take the time to know you and understand your needs.

2. *Life expectancy*: This factor goes along with age, but it deserves specific attention. If your life expectancy is short (ten to fifteen years or less) and you have substantial assets, do you really want to spend the rest of your days worrying about the market? Why would you? Every time we've seen a significant bear market over the past four decades, my oldest investors call to make sure they'll be okay. If they've chosen a balanced approach to investing, the answer is always *yes*. If they've insisted on going heavily into stocks, sometimes they have good reason to worry.

3. *Portfolio size*: The less you have to invest, the greater caution you must take to protect your capital. No matter how

you look at it, there is an element of risk to stock investment, and there's a big difference between putting your last $100,000 in the market versus putting $100,000 off the top of several million.

4. *Risk tolerance*: Truth is, no matter how much money you have or how smooth or rough the market, some people just never get comfortable with their exposure in stocks. The trouble here is that people who spend their days freaking out about every fluctuation in their investments tend to make decisions based on fear and greed—meaning they panic and sell when things get choppy, and they panic and buy when they fear they're missing a climb. Both of those things get them into trouble. If you find your emotional health is allergic to stock investment, then eventually your financial health will suffer, too. Alternately, if you know you can be steady in the face of market movement and feel comfortable taking more risk, it's okay to go a little deeper into stocks.

GOING STOCK-FREE

Many investors who have the most difficult time with stock investment are those who've always been in private business or in real estate—in things where they have more control. When your rental property isn't generating the income you want, you can paint it, you can change the price, you can replace a tenant, cut costs, etc. It's your party. But the stock market is bigger than you are, and you don't control anything about it. That, in a nutshell, is why some people who are in private business do not make good stock investors. The absence of a physical asset and a sense of control is more than they can tolerate. If this fits your profile, it's okay to say *No* to the market. You can make strides to offset inflation with income-producing real estate and investments in reliably profitable private businesses. You'll face the ongoing challenge of beating inflation, but you'll avoid the kinds of panic- or disgust-driven market mistakes that wipe out principal. For most investors, this isn't the most prudent path, but there are times when it's a viable solution.

OXBOW NOTE

In my book *Your Money Mentality: How You Feel About Risk, Losses, and Gains*, I explain that investing is not linear and how successful investment strategy must sometimes go against conventional wisdom. I walk investors through the highs and lows of the market to help them determine their individual money mentality. If you'd like a complimentary copy of this book, contact us at www.OxbowAdvisors.com.

CHAPTER 5

THE ROLE OF BONDS

Bonds are the investment world's essential defensive position. While they don't bring in dramatic returns, don't double or split or shoot the moon, they usually provide a reliable (if low) return. This makes them a critical component in any balanced investment strategy—especially because *most* of the time (though not *all* of the time) when stocks go up, bonds go down, and vice versa. When you look at investments from a long, historical perspective, stocks typically have the highest returns, then bonds, and finally treasury bills.

Depending on how you approach bond investment, it can be utilized with minimal risk. At Oxbow, for example, we're substantially invested in bonds with five-year-or-less maturities. In order to utilize this investment vehicle for both a steady return and ready cash, we keep them on a rolling rotation, buying new limited-term bonds as old ones come due. This practice protects principal in a way you simply can't manage on a twenty-five- or thirty-year note. On those long bonds, if rates go up substantially, you could conceivably lose just as much as you could in the stock market. On a two- or three-year bond, you're going to have your money back before that kind of hard loss comes into play.

THE FUNDAMENTALS: EQUITY VERSUS DEBT

The average investor thinks of bonds as uniformly and unequivocally safe, but that's an exaggeration. It's true that bonds are a different kind of commitment than stocks—lending money to a company rather than buying a piece of it—but it's still possible to lose out, especially if you put your assets into an entity that's not sound.

Another commonly overlooked factor of bond investment is the possibility that changing interest rates may impact value. When I first got into the investment business in the late 1970s, a number of my early advising clients were widows who'd bought bonds a decade or more earlier. Inflation was soaring (not unlike it did again starting in 2022), and as interest rates went up, the value of those bonds went down. It's a terrible thing to have to be the person explaining to an investor that the "safe" bonds they purchased long ago are now worth sixty cents on the dollar.

In 2022, as inflation took off, investors who owned thirty-year bonds lost somewhere in the neighborhood of 18 percent of their investment as rates went up. Again, those investors thought they were safe and were caught up short. So *yes*, bonds are generally a safer investment than stocks, but *no*, they're not a sure thing.

COMMON PITFALLS

Just like stocks (or any other investment vehicle), bonds have weak points. When it comes to these investments, there are a couple concerns of which every investor should be aware.

Falling behind inflation

The single biggest concern to consider in bond investment is that returns may not keep up with inflation. If you're earning 4 percent on your bond investment and inflation is 5 percent, you're just continuously falling behind. It may not sound like a big deal, but if you've created a level of wealth that generates enough income to support you, then keeping up with inflation may well mean the difference between living off your investments and having to spend down your capital.

Going the fund route

You've heard Forrest Gump say, "Life is like a box of chocolates. You never know what you're gonna get." Well, bond funds are the investment equivalent of a box of chocolates. Wall Street loves to push the premise of bond fund investment, but the fact is, quite often even the broker selling this package doesn't know exactly what's in it. And if you get into a long-term fund of mystery bonds and something goes awry, there's a good chance that same advisor won't be able to tell you how to handle it because of that factor.

A scrupulous, professional investment advisor knows the bonds they're buying. They don't get caught up in packaged and bundled bargains. Their investments are known entities, and if one of those takes a 4 or 5 percent drop for some reason, they'll be able to tell you what's going on and how best to maximize what you can get out of it.

Fixed returns

If you own straight bonds, you're likely locked into something that's not going to get any better. This is both the strength and the weakness of this investment tool: it'll get you a steady return, but it's never going to offer the big moments—or the big returns—that keep so many investors tuned in to the stock market's every move.

CHAPTER 6

THE CASE FOR CASH

The third (and often forgotten) essential component of a working and balanced investment portfolio is cash and cash equivalents—your "bulletproof" money. This is an overlooked aspect for many investors—one they ignore at their peril. In a rough market, we at Oxbow often carry a large percentage of cash as we wait for buys with good value to come into play. The fact is, there's always a rainy day coming. Every investor should recognize this fact and keep a cash buffer as a margin of safety.

You can trace a history of holding cash through some of the most successful investors and business owners in history. Bill Gates has often mentioned that when Microsoft was a young company, he set a rule that it would always have one year's payroll on hand—even if no payments came in. That conservative approach helped ensure the company's longevity.

Another renowned investor who's always respected the value of cash is Warren Buffett. Despite his oft-quoted statements about not trying to time the market, if you look back through Berkshire Hathaway's long history, you'll find they've shown great restraint and good timing with their cash reserves. Whether you call it timing the market or refusing to splurge on overvalued stocks, for example, it's no coincidence that the company was sitting on $129 *billion* in cash at the end of 2022.

In a time when stock buybacks have allowed significant manipulation of corporate value at the cost of corporate cash, this becomes more important than ever—both in managing your own investments and in choosing companies to trust with your money.

THE FUNDAMENTALS

When we talk about cash in this context, it's any investment vehicle that you could, if necessary, liquidate on any given day and get your money out without any loss of principal: floating treasuries, short-term CDs, savings, etc.—all the places where cash can sit safely.

This is a book about balance, and I promise you that if you speak with a Wall Street firm, they'll talk about balance, too. They'll give you a one-size-fits-all formula based on your age and perceived risk tolerance—maybe 60 percent stocks and 40 percent bonds—and they'll tell you you're going to be fine. *Unless*, of course, your money encounters any volatility.

Here's a news flash: if you had a portfolio with that 60/40 stocks/bonds blend in 2022, you lost more than in any other year in a century. Over the course of that devastatingly difficult year, we at Oxbow chose an entirely different kind of asset blend—one that started with 50 percent of assets in cash. Why? Because stock prices were sky-high and desperately overdue for a correction.

RESISTANCE IS COMMON

Over the years, I've often had pushback from investors who believe assets held as cash are being wasted, but you don't have to look any further than the most financially successful individuals and companies to see that's just not true. For example, several years ago I interviewed a number of billionaires while writing my book *The Psychology of Staying Rich*. One topic we explored at length was the importance of cash. On average, these largest-scale investors held 30 percent of their assets in cash on any given day. Notably, when I asked why, almost every one said that when times get tough in an industry or in the overall economy, they're always ready to make money. The expression "cash is king" isn't just talk. If you want to be ready to scoop up the best bargains, you've got to have liquidity to make it happen.

Many of those bargains come along during the couple of times each decade when the markets inevitably get truly beaten down. When it happens, while most people are running away from stocks, those who've been patiently waiting for an ideal time to start buying step forward and very quickly gain ground.

If you keep your eyes open long enough in the investment business, you learn to look for these opportunities. In 2003 and 2009, for example, Oxbow's investors had very good years. Why? Because when the economy goes through a bear market—a long one—the return average in the first year that follows ranges from 43 to 68 percent. The only way you get to partake in that—at a time when most people have become repulsed at the very idea of stock investment—is if you have both the presence of mind and the cash on hand to capitalize on the opportunity.

Cash is an equally powerful tool in taking advantage of other buy-in opportunities, including investing in real estate and in private businesses.

The absence of cash, on the other hand, leads to fear—to examining *What if?* scenarios and seeing the potential for dreadful outcomes. When you're fearful, you're also distrustful, and neither of those emotions are conducive to wise investment decisions.

That's why it's so important to get your portfolio in balance and keep it that way.

CASH = SECURITY

If you're on the fence about holding cash, consider the examples of some of the best public companies on the market. In a year like 2022, when markets faltered, public companies that don't actually make any money were doomed to fail. They had no backup, no net to break their fall. Truth is, the lifeblood of any investment is cash flow, and if you scrutinize any truly great business, you'll find they have cash in their pocket to draw on in tough times. They may not know what revenues are going to be in an upcoming quarter, but they do know they're going to weather whatever comes. That's simple, sound business practice—and it's simple, sound investment practice as well.

It's invariably at the worst times that the truth comes out about who hasn't been careful to keep a cash cushion. As Warren Buffett famously said, "Only when the tide goes out do you learn who has been swimming naked."

Over the years, I've met several keen business owners who sold their companies and promptly forgot the critical importance of holding some cash. When you put everything you have to work in investments and leave your pockets empty, you leave yourself vulnerable. When something comes up for which these over-leveraged investors need money, they'll need to have a fire sale in one area or another of their portfolio. In the long run, situations that require capital ASAP are inescapable. Those who plan for them by keeping cash as an essential part of their investment plan won't have to sweat them.

It's worth noting that while the buying power of cash is a key reason to hold it, at the end of the day it's the psychological security that comes with knowing a portion of your assets are invulnerable that makes all the difference. There's no spending or saving profile that won't benefit from being mindful of this measure of safety.

Think of it this way: investing is so much about controlling your emotions. It's extremely hard to do that if you don't have any cash. It's a common misconception that the role of an expert financial advisor is solely focused on numbers. In truth, the job equally requires the ability to sit down with people, to understand the emotions driving their financial decisions, to respect their priorities, and then to help them make investments that will ensure their peace of mind. Cash must always be part of that conversation.

HOW MUCH IS ENOUGH?
HOW MUCH IS TOO MUCH?

What percentage of your assets should be bulletproof? In a balanced market, somewhere in the neighborhood of 15–25 percent. In a down market, significantly more. At Oxbow, we typically hold an average of 15–20 percent in cash, with a bare minimum of 10 percent. Everyone needs at least that. Investors with smaller portfolios are often fixated on the idea of keeping all their money working all the time. This group, however, is the one that can least afford to tie up all their liquidity. What's more, if you look at historical data, you'll consistently find that it is small investors who are ducking out of the market at its lows rather than buying in.

For bigger investors—say those with assets over $50 million— the floor should be higher, in the ballpark of 20 percent. If you reach a point where your wealth will support your lifestyle for the rest of your life, there really is no excuse for getting into a position where you could lose that.

Even in investing, there is a season for everything, and one of the toughest lessons individual investors have been learning through all history is that sometimes they need to simply watch and wait.

It's important to note that this is a lesson many investment advisors are still working to learn as well. Consider the fact that in 2023, roughly half the people active in the industry had only been in the business since the last market low. They'd never had the opportunity to manage funds during a lasting bear market, and, even more remarkably, they'd never encountered significant inflation. I have a great deal of respect for the intellects and educations of our youngest generations of professional advisors, but they must work twice as hard to understand historical data when they've had precious few experiences to teach them how to advise through tough financial times.

OXBOW NOTE

Strange as it may sound, holding on to wealth often turns out to be even harder for families than getting it in the first place. The majority of wealthy Americans fail to keep their fortunes in the family for more than a single generation—and many don't make it that far. If you'd like a free copy of *The Psychology of Staying Rich: How to Preserve Wealth and Establish an Enduring Financial Legacy*, contact us at www.OxbowAdvisors.com.

CHAPTER 7

THE OXBOW WAY: THE HIGH-INCOME PORTFOLIO

In 1992, my group of advisors set out to develop an investment strategy that would bridge the gap between those who hoped for (but could not rely on) significant cash flow from stock investments and those who didn't want to be in the stodgy part of the bond market. Many of these investors—then and to this day—were former business owners with extensive experience managing both companies and money. They, like our team, knew there must be a better way than just allocating between the stock and bond markets. With that in mind, we created a high-income category of investments—a class that was safer than stocks but more lucrative than bonds. Our minimum benchmark has always been to beat the bond market and bring in returns at moderate risk to our investors. For the most part, the strategy has always been able to deliver.

THE FUNDAMENTALS

New investors with Oxbow are always interested in this strategy, with good reason, and so we have plenty of opportunities to explain the nuts and bolts of it. What kinds of investments make the cut to be considered "high income"? For starters, we look for investments that will pay 2–4 percent more than common stocks. Our selections include preferred and convertible stocks and bonds, gas pipelines and other energy investments, and real estate investment trusts—many of which have increases built into their terms. The choices are expertly made to bring in yields of 5–10 percent. So if the stock market goes up 20 percent or more, it's not going to match that. But if the market drops, it typically beats it. What's more, the high-income strategy does a better job of keeping pace with and beating inflation than bond investments.

We created this strategy because our business owners and former business owners expected cash flow with less risk than the general market, and we knew we had the expertise to meet that objective.

In an extremely tough period across financial markets, sometimes the best an investor can expect is to mitigate loss, and the high-income strategy does that, too. Over the course of 2022, for example, the S&P lost nearly 20 percent, the NASDAQ lost more than 33 percent, and the 10-year US Treasury bond market lost over 18 percent. By comparison, Oxbow's high-income account far outperformed any of those numbers. Anytime you look at investment losses, you're assessing how quickly you'll be able to recover as conditions change. I can tell you with certainty that if you have a less-than-5-percent drop, you can recover extremely quickly. But 20 or more percent? That poses a bigger and longer challenge. Many investors fail to understand just how long it can take to turn their losses around before they can start seeing returns again.

AN ESSENTIAL DIFFERENCE

Because so many of Oxbow's investors are former business owners, they are an exceptionally savvy group when it comes to the questions they ask about their money management and their expectations for it. Most also arrive with strong opinions about investments in general and in how they want their fortunes protected and grown. That's all great as long as they're also ready to listen and learn a new field, because investing is both a science and an art, and neither can be learned overnight or just by getting a subscription to *The Wall Street Journal*.

The number one issue that arises early in these relationships is comfort level with risk. Some people just cannot handle it—and many of those individuals don't discover that fact until they take their first loss. At Oxbow, the conversations we have before investing a dime of your money and the choices we ask investors to make as they consider our strategies are all designed to get a handle on risk tolerance sooner than later. You can always get more aggressive over time if you choose, but you can't put the genie back in the bottle if you take a drubbing in your first year of high-risk choices.

Oxbow's high-income portfolio is targeted for the investor who sold a business in that it recognizes the value of that experience. Most of our investors own real estate. Most of them have employees. Many have built something from very little, and some have even reached a point where they have to answer to a board and justify their financial and managerial choices. These are people who have been forged by accountability throughout their careers—whether it came in the form of having to meet payroll or having to earn new investors and expanded contracts. It's no wonder some of them look at the stock market, shake their heads, and say, "I don't understand that, and I'll never do it."

Conversely, some of these individuals have been so flush with success and good fortune that they've forgotten things can go wrong. They're the ones who look at the stock market and say, "Sign me up. I'll put everything on X, Y, and Z stock." They're in for a different kind of lesson because in the investment world, being smart and lucky just isn't enough when you're dealing in markets that feel ripples from events and actions in every industry and every locality around the world.

These factors—histories of excellence and the particular vulnerabilities of being new to high-dollar investment—are always on the minds of our team as we select and oversee high-income strategy investments, making it our job to find that rich middle ground between high-stakes and low-return options.

Part 3

STRATEGY
IN MOTION

CHAPTER 8

THE RIGHT MIX FOR YOU

No matter what components go into an investment strategy, there is no across-the-board formula—just like there's no single Holy Grail investment that works for everyone. Instead, you've got to factor in your risk tolerance, income needs, age, and financial goals. As you do so, you can't just plan for good times. That's just *hoping*, not planning.

At Oxbow, we encourage investors to find balance between three general strategies: a conservative fixed-income strategy, our proprietary high-income strategy, and an aggressive stock-heavy strategy. Going all in on any of these is not advisable. Instead, investors should find the right balance for their needs among them. For some that's simply a third in each strategy, but for others the balance may be skewed toward more aggressive or conservative investments. Consider the components of each:

1. *Conservative fixed-income strategy*: This is the slow-and-steady category, focused first on the safety and reliability of its components. These investments include short-term maturities and low-volatility, high-quality assets. This strategy matches well with base capital—with money you don't intend to put at risk because it's essential to your lifetime living costs. Almost all of our investors have some assets in this strategy.

2. *High-income strategy*: This category is aggressively designed to beat the bond market without taking on the level of risk inherent in a strictly stock portfolio. It includes a number of asset classes and types of securities within those classes. Everything in this strategy has to pay above-average income to meet its standards. Many of these are out-of-the-box investments that are easily overlooked by individual investors. For example, investment trusts that own real estate leases—not only are these investments relatively secure compared to the stock market, but, critically, they have increased income built into their contracts. That helps ensure they'll consistently outpace standard bond returns.

3. *Stock strategy*: This category was developed to foster long-term growth. It's focused on owning companies that can grow above average for a long period of time. These investments aren't in just any stock but in companies with low debt and a lot of cash on their balance sheets. They must be in a position to keep profit margins high. At Oxbow, we choose companies we can own for many years. A lot of people will buy a great company but sell it too early. Others own companies that have peaked and flopped, but they don't want to let them go.

Our longest-held stock is a perfect example of the stock strategy in action. We've owned Microsoft for eighteen years at the time of this writing. Our original cost was in the ballpark of $15 per share. As it got higher, we kept our position but took profits. We did that steadily along the way, including when the stock hit an all-time high near $350 per share in 2021. As the stock has pulled back, we've been comfortable with our position for two reasons: first because we've already made money on it time and again as we sold it on the way up, and second because the company has, to date, shown itself worthy of our investment. Individual investors rarely demonstrate such a measured approach—they get emotionally invested and are all in (or all out) on their choices.

SLOW-ROLL STARTS

Typically, the first question a new investor asks about these strategies is whether they beat the market. This is the wrong question. Beating the market isn't the goal. The goal is beating inflation and matching investments with each person's individual risk parameters. This is not a game; it's the protection of hard-earned assets.

The next question that belies skewed priorities has to do with how quickly assets can be deployed and put to work. It's never a good idea to dive headfirst into a new investment strategy. Instead, I recommend easing in and getting comfortable with the level of risk you've chosen. A long, slow infusion into your preferred investments will give you some psychological breathing room, and it'll help mitigate any concerns about poor market timing.

If you came into the market in January of 2021 and got returns that were much higher than the norm, for example, then you'd be wise to hold off a little bit. In hindsight, 2022 between the S&P 500 and the Nasdaq Composite were down combined—25 percent. Get the picture? You're immediately skewed on your average return. A wise advisor will share the average return for the market for one year, five years, and ten years. If you're above that number, slow down, because these things almost inevitably come back to the mean. This can be hard for investors to accept, but if you're going to work the markets, you must understand at the most elemental level that they will go down as well as up.

Too often I've seen investors who are fortunate enough to

come into the market during a couple bang-up years posting huge average returns go off and ruin it. The great entry point is excellent news for them—right up until they get hooked and insist on staying 100 percent in it.

Here's how it plays out in real numbers: let's say you took a million dollars and invested well with good timing in 1997. You made 20 percent each year for three years. Bravo—at that point your million dollars was worth $1.7 million (minus taxes).

Throughout that process and in the aftermath you faced a choice: hang on and hope, or take a profit and reallocate to other, safer investments or to cash. Most people who've had that kind of success are sorely tempted to stay all in, but let's look at the next couple years. If you'd kept your $1.7 million fully invested after your big gain, then by February of 2003 you would have lost $950,000 of it.

Bottom line? You'd be 20 percent down despite all your early success.

You might argue that's just the way the market works, but that flies in the face of balance. If you'd taken a balanced approach, you'd have held less and lost less. Let's look a little deeper at that.

PERPETUAL BALANCE

Perhaps the most important thing to know about portfolio balance is that it's not just a one-and-done activity. Over time, investors must revisit their choices in each strategy to ensure continued balance. For example, consider an investor who chooses to put a third of their assets in each class. If this individual starts with $21 million and puts $7 million in each strategy, then as the assets in each rise or fall, they go back and rebalance at regular intervals. If your conservative fund goes up to $7.5 million, your high income goes to $8 million, and your stock portfolio drops to $6 million, then the point will come when you'll want to reallocate so the funds are balanced again.

Why make a practice of reallocating? Because investors are so often backward-looking and fickle in their choices. They look at what's happened lately and make moves to hop on trends that are nearly over. In doing so, they can easily miss out on years of good stock returns and then dive into the market just in time for a drop. Staying balanced protects not just against disproportionate losses but also against missing out on gains.

PITFALLS: DUDS AND FADS

One of the most common failings of out-of-balance investors is clinging to dud stocks and chasing after flash-in-the-pan fads. The wise investor is aware of both and makes a point to stay clear.

When it comes to duds, these are the stocks investors become attached to and get in a rut with. Many have paid out in the past—but then tread water for decades. At best this is ineffective, but at worst it ties up assets that could be deployed to great effect in other ways. There are countless examples of this. Consider Proctor & Gamble. In 1998, a person could have bought this stock for a little under $60 per share. Fourteen years later, it was still trading at the same price. A more recent market took it higher, but it is an all-too-common theme in investing that people cling to stocks that haven't made them a dime in ten or fifteen or twenty years. Some people will say the stocks they own won't go down. Or they look at a 3 percent dividend and call it good. But all stocks go down eventually. And that 3 percent dividend isn't the reason you buy and hold. It doesn't even match inflation.

The second common investment failure that deserves mention here is fads. These are as much a fact of life in money as they are in fashion or home decor. At one point, you've got bell-bottom jeans and Formica countertops, and a few years later you can't stand the sight of either. Wall Street is the biggest purveyor of investment fads, selling them as gleaming opportunities. It's the reason cigars became a hot investment in 1997–98. It's the reason internet stocks soared leading up to 2000 (and for that matter that the crazy Beanie Babies bubble happened right alongside them). This is also the reason unregulated cryptocurrencies—which are shaping up to earn a place among history's most impressive money-making schemes—were able to gain enough momentum coming into 2022 to wipe out billions of dollars by year's end.

The fact is, nobody even whispered to those investors that they might be getting in on the financial equivalent of the Chia Pet.

When it comes to investment, just like in most fields, investors should beware trendy options that aren't underpinned by profitable companies that provide a good or service, that have and make money, and that are capable of long-term growth. If your potential investment doesn't meet those criteria, it fails the sniff test.

OXBOW NOTE

First-generation wealth earners need to constantly guard against schemes designed to separate them from their money. These tests of your judgment don't always come in the form of shady characters with questionable reputations. Many show up polished, with the sheen of Wall Street on them. Just remember the caveat of *buyer beware*. If you'd like a free copy of Oxbow's analysis of this topic, *Wall Street Lies: 5 Myths to Keep Your Money in Their Game*, contact us at www.OxbowAdvisors.com.

CHAPTER 9

EXCEPTIONS TO THE RULES—TWO TIMES TO CHOOSE IMBALANCE

This whole book has been about a balanced portfolio. This is definitely the way to a steady and consistent investment approach. But there are two situations where an investor may choose to be over-allocated. Let's take a look at each of them.

AT MARKET LOWS

The question of the ages is this: *Where is the bottom?* Or more specifically, *Where is the low point worthy of taking more risk?* There is no crystal ball that will give you a specific number, but there are ranges that can serve as signs to buy.

For example, as the stock market falls, selling intensifies. When you see the S&P 500 or the Dow Jones Industrial Average down between −25 to −50 percent, that's the time to start thinking about more stock exposure. In particular, when averages get into the −35 percent area, it may be time to move more into stocks or equity. History will tell you the worst bear markets have gone down −50 percent on average—and that many times the last part of the move comes quickly. You can't pinpoint the bottom, but if you buy stocks at, say, −40 percent and a little more if they keep falling, you're positioning yourself for the rise. At this stage you aren't trying to be all stocks, but you are trying to beef up exposure by, say, 20 percent in the stock market. If you are confused on which stocks, then you can choose to buy the index average.

Be aware that in most cases your investment will go down from where you bought it for a short time. Negative markets keep the selling going until everyone is washed out. I often tell people that one true sign of a market reaching bottom is when it seems like everyone around you is utterly disgusted at even the thought of stocks. As the saying goes, *It's always darkest before the light.*

You may not be able to hit a specific point, but you can put yourself in the zone. Case in point: at Oxbow we started pushing more money into stocks toward the very end of 2008. The Dow was over 14,000 in October of 2007, then fell to around 8,500 in December of 2008. That was a whopping –39 percent drop. Obviously we felt good about coming in at that point. But two months into 2009, the market had fallen to 6,700—another –20 percent. I remember sitting in my hotel in Dallas with a copy of *The Wall Street Journal*—a copy I still have today. It was dated Tuesday, March 3, 2009. Even after a lifetime of being in this business, I was forced to face the fear I talk other investors through every day. *Was the buy-in a mistake?*

Turns out it wasn't. Fifteen months later the Dow was at 10,000. We had successfully navigated the wider trend of a potentially devastating downturn and recovery.

AT MARKET HIGHS

Everyone asks how to know when it's time to decrease your exposure to the stock market. I can't give you a number, but I can certainly tell you a little about the road signs. Start to watch normal business metrics to get an idea of excess. For instance, using the S&P 500, find out the average price-to-earnings multiple and where that is relative to historical numbers. Also look at price-to-sales. Two-and-a-half to three times is getting expensive.

Watch some tried-and-true measures, like the Value Line survey that shows expected return over the next three to five years. The guidelines seem simple, but they've proven to be useful guideposts over the long run.

Even though the market may go higher (and probably will), these numbers indicate it's time to unbalance a bit and have more cash. You may feel as though you made an error as the market tries to go higher. Case in point: in April of 1999, with the Dow Jones Industrial Average at 10,500, at Oxbow we sold our last tech stock and raised a lot of cash. We thought the stock market was in a bubble. At that time every metric was off-the-charts expensive. Ten months later the Dow Jones hit 11,500, and we had a lot of questions to answer. But fast-forward to October 2001, and the Dow stood at 8,000. These things take time to sort themselves out, but if you can recognize when you are in a bubble, you have the opportunity to balance toward safety.

LOOK TO THE FUTURE AND REST EASY

A t the core of any investment advice that helps you get into balance and stay there is this: allocate your assets in well-defined tiers. The lowest level of these, the base, is liquid. It takes the form of cash and extremely safe holdings you can get your money out of at-will. These are the funds you *know* you're not going to lose. It's your rest-easy money, sufficient to cover your living expenses for a long period of time.

Second-tier money belongs in low-risk investments like bonds and can sometimes spread over into the kinds of income-producing-but-stable options I shared in chapter 7 about the Oxbow Way. These assets are working for you, but they're not nearly as volatile as funds in the stock market.

Third-tier money belongs in stock investments—not in wildly fluctuating pseudo-corporations and of-the-moment trends, but in well-managed, stable, consistently profitable companies. For those who can't stomach stocks, this tier may include income-producing real estate or private company investments.

Some people who really want to explore possibilities create a fourth, smallest tier. This one can be used for discretionary investments in things like promising-but-unproven private companies or more speculative stocks. If the rest of your money is well allocated, this is an area where you have room to stretch without putting the principal you intend to use to support your lifestyle indefinitely at risk.

Your peace of mind comes down to the fact that if one of these tiers is hard at work for you and another drops, you'll be fine. Even if two of the three briefly take a beating (as happened in 2022 in both stocks and bonds), you maintain your base liquidity—and therefore also your buying power. By regularly reassessing and reallocating, you keep in balance, keep the ability to weather any storm, and keep your wealth working for you and your family.

ABOUT THE AUTHOR

J. TED OAKLEY, founder and managing partner of Oxbow Advisors, began his career in the investment industry in 1976. The Oxbow Principles and the firm's proprietary investment strategies are founded on the unique perspective he has gained during his decades-long tenure advising high–net worth investors. Ted's investment advice provides principled guidance to investors from more than half the states in the US. He frequently counsels former business owners on protecting and wisely investing their newly liquid wealth. Ted is the author of several other books, including the following:

- *Your Money Mentality: How You Feel About Risk, Losses, and Gains*

- *You Sold Your Company: Get Ready for Change*

- *$20 Million and Broke: If You Have It, Don't Lose It*

- *The Psychology of Staying Rich: How to Preserve Wealth and Establish an Enduring Financial Legacy*

- *Danger Time: The 2–3 Year Red Zone after Selling Your Company*

- *Rich Kids, Broke Kids: The Failure of Traditional Estate Planning*

- *Crazy Time: Surviving the First 12 Months after Selling Your Company*

- *My Story: From Poor Kid to Business Owner*

- *Wall Street Lies: 5 Myths to Keep Your Cash in Their Game,* with Pat Swanson and Trey Crain